FUTUROPOLIS

1. The Lunar Base by Leslie Carr, based on a
drawing by R A Smith.

ROBERT SHECKLEY
FUTUROPOLIS

BERGSTRÖM+BOYLE/BIG O/LONDON

This edition published in 1979 by Big O Publishing Ltd.,
219 Eversleigh Road, London SW11 5UY
Telephone 01-228 3392, Telex 914549

Produced and published by
Bergström and Boyle Books Limited
31 Foubert's Place, London W1, England

Designed by Tamasin Cole

Original artwork by David Austin

Production services by
Book Production Consultants,
7 Brooklands Avenue, Cambridge, England

Typesetting by Bedford Typesetters Limited,
Bedford, England

Made and printed in Hong Kong by
Mandarin Publishers Limited,
22a Westlands Road, Quarry Bay, Hong Kong

ISBN 0 903767 22 8

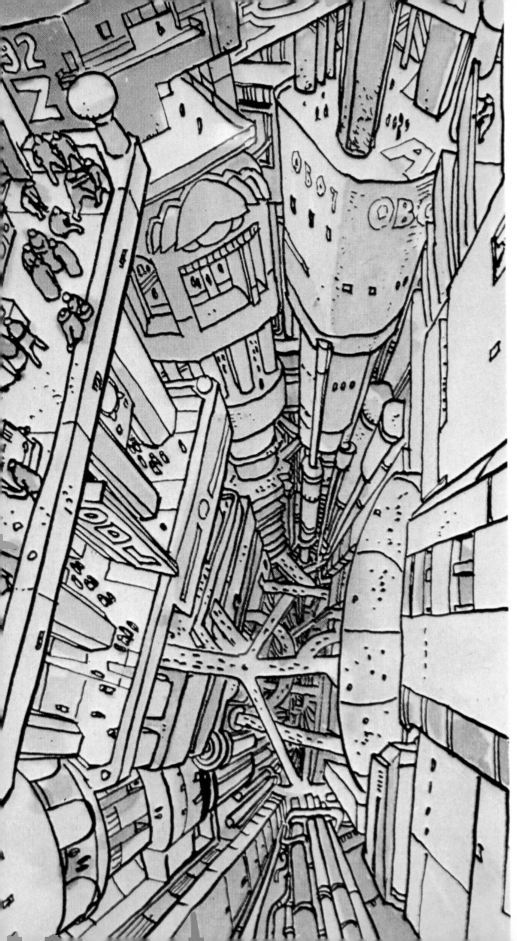

CONTENTS

Introduction

Constructions of Hell

Asteroid Developers are pleased to
announce . . .

Can my city come visit your city ?

I have seen the future and it's fun

Acknowledgments

2. A fiendish cityscape by French artist Moebius
from The Long Tomorrow by Dan O'Bannon.

3. Alexander the Great's architect Dinocrates devised this colossal project. Mount Athos was to be carved into the image of a man, with one arm extended to hold a water reservoir to supply the city built in his lap and around his nether limbs.

'The city is a fact in nature, like a cave, a run of mackerel or an ant-heap. But it is also a conscious work of art, and it holds within its communal framework many simpler and more personal forms of art. Mind takes form in the city; and in turn, urban forms condition mind. For space, no less than time, is artfully reorganized in cities: in boundary lines and silhouettes, in the fixing of horizontal planes and vertical peaks, in utilizing or denying the natural site, the city records the attitude of a culture and an epoch to the fundamental facts of its existence. The dome and the spire, the open avenue and the closed court, tell the story, not merely of different physical accommodations, but of essentially different conceptions of man's destiny. The city is both a physical utility for collective living and a symbol of those collective purposes and unanimities that arise under such favoring circumstance. With language itself, it remains man's greatest work of art.'

Lewis Mumford, The Culture of Cities, **p 5.**

4. Continuous Monument, an architect's idea of total urbanization – a city that extends around the world. Superstudio, 1970.

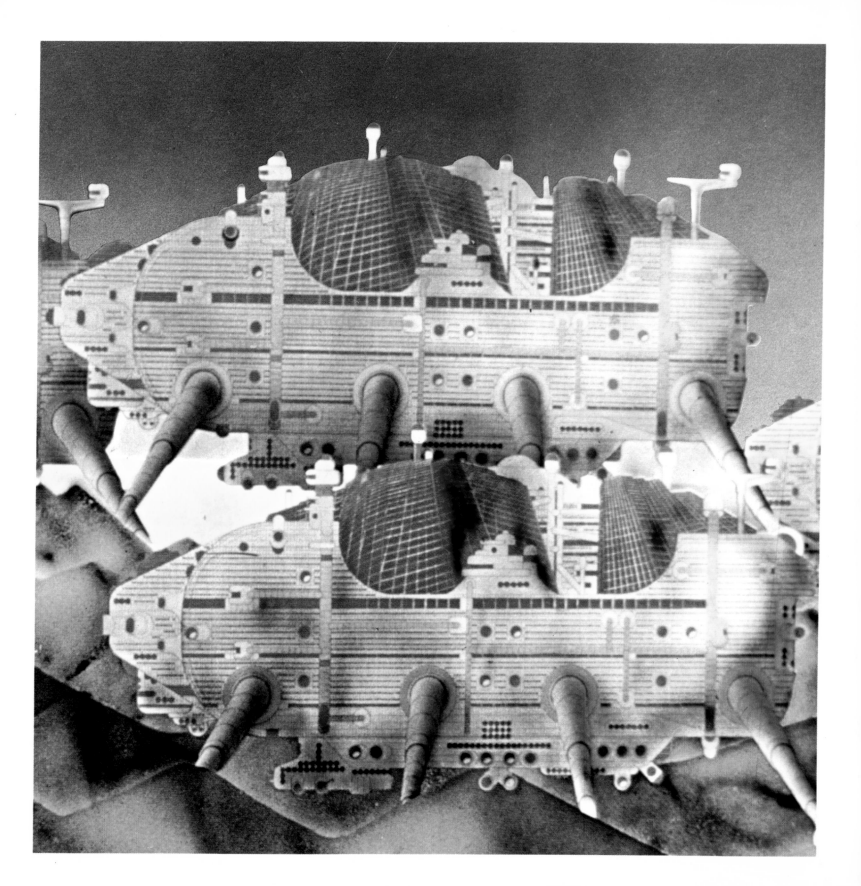

'For I dipt into the future, far as human eye could see,
Saw the Vision of the world, and all the wonder that would be;

Saw the heavens fill with commerce, argosies of magic sails,
Pilots of the purple twilight, dropping down with costly bales;

Heard the heavens fill with shouting, and there rain'd a ghastly dew
From the nations' airy navies grappling, in the central blue;

Far along the world-wide whisper of the south-wind rushing warm,
With the standards of the peoples plunging thro' the thunder storm;

Till the war-drum throbb'd no longer, and the battle-flags were furl'd
In the Parliament of man, the Federation of the world.

There the common sense of most shall hold a fretful realm in awe,
And the kindly earth shall slumber, lapt in universal law.'

Locksley Hall, **Alfred Lord Tennyson.**

5.   Walking City **by Ron Herron.**

Men have been planning Futuropolis for a long time, and in many different ways. It is a vast and diverse subject. This book takes a look at some of the visions, both celestial and infernal, that men have had concerning their cities. Our selections range from Plato's 'Republic' to modern science fiction.

The ability to live dramatically is the peculiar talent of our species. The city provides a frame for our endeavors, a platform for our thoughts, and a stage on which the tragi-comic actions of our lives are acted out. It is the basis for nearly all our culture. Without it, art and science could not exist. History, too would be impossible without the continuity of city life. The city is our own unique product. It cannot properly be likened to anything else in nature.

Two main currents of thought characterize the planning of Futuropolis. They are the utopian and the dystopian outlooks. The utopian view has been expressed by many serious philosophers and social reformers. It is characterized by earnestness. It takes the direct approach to prescribing to our condition. Most utopias would not be pleasant places to live in.

6. Buon governo in città **by Lorenzetti.**

Modern science fiction tends to the dystopian view. Science fiction cities either do not work very well or they work much too well for comfort. They are impressionistic rather than realistic. You are not meant to start appropriating land for a science fiction city. Its function is to suggest what you should avoid rather than what you should include.

What will Futuropolis be like? We may be able to put our city together and take it apart like a doll's house. Perhaps we will put it on wheels or rails, locate it under the sea or out in space. We might even dispense with any formal structure and carry individual sections of our city around with us, to plug in where we please. There are almost limitless possibilities. And of course, the planning of Futuropolis reveals our conflicts and uncertainties as well as our hopes and dreams. To speculate on the future is to express what is wrong with our present life.

7. Inside these vast oxygen tents the air might be sterile — but what about the quality of life? Frei Otto's projected design for the Medical Academy at Ulm, three large interconnected glass cones covering 8,500 square metres.

Facing page
8. Tower of Babel **by Pieter Breughel the Elder.**

One of the earliest planned cities on record is Kahune in Egypt. It dates from 2500 BC, and was built to house workers for the construction of the nearby pyramid of Illahun. The city was occupied for only twenty-one years. Nobody liked it. It was a hell city.

Hell cities are the ones that didn't work out. They are the miscalculations, the mistakes. No one planned for them to come out that way, but they did. Science fiction has done extensive exploration into various dystopian possibilities, and has come up with a few things we might think about as we plan our garden cities of the future.

The prime dystopian theme of our time is overpopulation. In Harry Harrison's recent novel, Make Room, Make Room, we find an anthology of the ills of that situation. The story takes place in a monstrously swollen New York of 1999. The police maintain a tenuous control over a desperate populace of mobs and special-interest groups. Filth chokes the streets, there are no jobs, even artificial foods are running out, water is rationed, and there is no hope in sight.

If the city survives or circumvents overcrowding, it is still in danger because of its sheer complexity. In J. G. Ballard's High Rise, we see a closeup view of the accelerated breakdown of an upper middle class garden apartment. As the power fails, as the elevators and other services break down, never to be fixed, the high-rise is transformed into a primitive cliff dwelling, and its brutalized inhabitants turn easily to murder and rape.

In E. M. Forster's The Machine Stops, we see push-button living taken to the ultimate degree. The city itself takes care of everyone's life. All citizens are free to live passively, in self-chosen isolation, in the pursuit of amusing ideas. This complex and decadent city begins spontaneously to disintegrate, perhaps as a symbol of the outcome of man's alienation from nature.

11.   J G Ballard's terrifying science fiction novel High Rise vividly describes the collapse of a society when its technology breaks down.

Facing page
10.   **Illustration by Colin Hay for** Lathe of Heaven.

Right

12. Idealized hell city of the future built on a 'silo' motif. The pollution problem has not been solved, but this does not matter. There are no people.

Below right

13. Space Shuttle, **by Bob Layzell.**

Below

14. Humanity must be subservient to productivity in the industrial zone development at Magnitogorsk in the Southern Urals, conceived and built in the early thirties.

15. Fire Time **by Colin Hay.**

16. Did he jump or was he pushed? Another human being fades into ant-like insignificance among the relentless high-rise blocks of a 1930's futuristic story.

In considering the shape of future cities, science-fiction examines those by whom they will be ruled, since this dictates their style. The political question is fundamental.

Orwell's conclusion in Nineteen Eighty-four is that the city of the future will be a police state. It is a common theme, and goes back at least as far as Plato, who found it desirable:

'It will be for the rulers of our city, then, if anyone, to use falsehood in dealing with citizen or enemy for the good of the State; no one else must do so. And if any citizen lies to our rulers, we shall regard it as a still graver offense than it is for a patient to lie to his doctor, or for an athlete to lie to his trainer about his physical condition, or for a sailor to misrepresent to his captain any matter concerning the ship or crew, or the state of himself or his fellow sailors.'

Plato, The Republic, part 3, 389c.

A police state is one in which other people tell you what to do and when to do it. If they are wrong about something, they apologize. If you are wrong about something, they kill you. Somehow it is not quite unbearable, which must explain why it lasts so long. A police state can be ruled by a king, a feudal council, an intellectual elite, or anyone else. The only qualification for ruling a police state is whether or not the police obey you. What counts is the will to disenfranchise the citizens for their own good; to legislate morality; to make all decisions in terms of the good of your state, or the glory of God, or the splendor of the king, or anything except the present and immediate welfare of the people.

Facing page
17. Views of the deluge. London Bridge is falling down, though London Transport struggles to keep going. Other world capitals do not escape the consequences of an encounter with the Red · Moon.

EAGLE-BRITAIN'S NATIONAL STRIP CARTOON WEEKLY

FOURPENCE-
HALFPENNY

EVERY FRIDAY

EAGLE

25 APRIL 1952 Vol. 3 No. 3

DAN DARE
THE RED MOON MYSTERY

For New Readers

The Earth's attack with atom bombs on Asteroid 2345, the Red Moon, has failed to change its course and it has started to circle the Earth. Its disruptive effect on the Earth's magnetic field causes terrible electrical storms and other disturbances. On the afternoon of Oct. 4th, 1999, it looms over a London partly submerged by a tidal wave roaring up the Thames.

GOSH! — LOOK WHAT'S COMING NOW — GOOD OLD LONDON TRANSPORT!

I WON'T ARGUE ABOUT THE FARE THIS TRIP.

AND SIMULTANEOUSLY THE REST OF THE WORLD REELS UNDER THE BLOWS OF THE FIRST ORBIT OF THE MYSTERIOUS RED GLOBE.

NEW YORK CALLING EMERGENCY CONTROL. THE LAST TREMOR SURE SHOOK THINGS UP! MANHATTAN ISN'T AN ISLAND ANY MORE — THE EAST RIVER'S DRY AS A BONE . . .

ALLEZ! VITE LA — TREMBLE- MENT DE TERRE!"

PAS DE CALAIS
CROIX + ROUGE
AMBULANCE

Above left
18. Soria y Mata's 1882 Lineal City, showing Madrid's Central Avenue prolonged indefinitely.

Middle left
19. According to Le Corbusier, three million people could live in this city.

Below left
20. Rigidly patterned town planning of the thirties in the USSR.

Above
21. Albert Speer's plan for Berlin, showing the three-mile avenue dominating the city.

Another sort of police state is the religious tyranny. This is preferable to the political variety, at least on the basis of style. A good example of this is seen in Fritz Leiber's fine novel, Gather, Darkness! In Megatheopolis, a city of Earth's future, a corrupt priesthood overawes the masses with scientific marvels disguised as religious miracles. It is a bad situation; but at least the citizens live in an architecturally impressive place, and get to see a lot of dazzling spectacles.

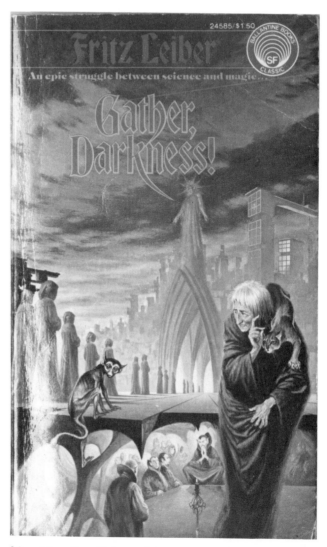

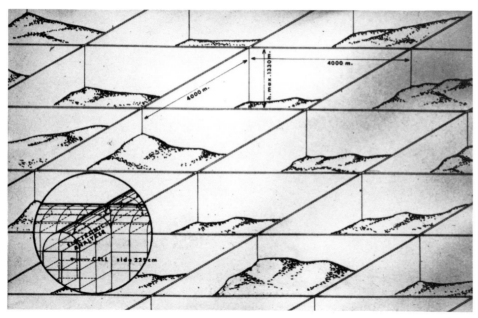

22. 2,000 Ton City, composed of cells each containing an individual whose brain impulses are continuously transmitted to an analyser which compares, selects and interprets the desires of each individual, programming the life of the entire city moment by moment. Each inhabitant lives eternally, but if he formulates thoughts of rebellion against this perfect life twice consecutively, the ceiling descends to crush him with its 2,000 ton force. Superstudio.

23. The fiendish architecture and grim inhabitants of the world of Fritz Leiber's Gather, Darkness!

Right
24. This 1920's vision of town planning tries to glamorize the elevated railroad system which was discarded in the United States by the mid-50s. The monorail in the foreground still has some relevance, however.

25. View of an Ideal City, by Piero della Francesca.

While considering the possible rulers of Futuropolis, we must not leave out the city itself. A city is a machine for living, and machines are getting smarter every year. Link the city with the computer and you get Automatic Hell City—a place that makes all of your decisions for you, usually for your own good and usually to your detriment. Still, as dystopias go, Automatic Hell City is not too bad a place to live. The computer is not cruel or capricious. It wants to be fair. Its only power is that which humans invest it with, as the hero of Forster's Machine Stops points out:

'Cannot you see, cannot all you lecturers see, that it is we that are dying, and that down here the only thing that really lives is the Machine? We created the Machine, to do our will, but we cannot make it do our will now. It has robbed us of the sense of space and of the sense of touch, it has blurred every human relation and narrowed down love to a carnal act, it has paralysed our bodies and our wills, and now it compels us to worship it.'

Yet the Machine is only serving mankind to the best of its abilities, following the false assumptions programmed into it. In Henry Kuttner's well known short story, Jesting Pilot, the City has been programmed to lie to the inhabitants, in order to conceal from them the reality of their situation. It does this 'for their own good', because the true reality is unbearable. But the reality that it is protecting them from is the sensory impact of the city itself.

In the early sixties, the Japanese architect Kenzo Tange detailed a project to allow Tokyo to expand by building over Tokyo Bay.

Above
26. A general view of the Bay, showing the linear spine containing 60% of floor area given to service and industries.

Below
27. Detail of the residential megastructures with internal recreation areas, garages and schools.

Cities of Tomorrow

The city of tomorrow, engineers say, will tend first to vastness; gigantic buildings connected by wide, suspended roadways on which traffic will speed at unheard of rates. This is the city the artist has pictured here. Traffic handled in huge underground tunnels, aerial ways, and in the air itself. Helicopter planes, capable of maneuvering about between buildings and roof-top airports, will take the place of the ground taxi. Each building will be virtually a city in itself, completely self-sustaining, receiving its supplies from great merchandise ways far below the ground. Dwellers and workers in these buildings may go weeks without setting foot on the ground, or the ground-level. In this city smoke will be eliminated, noise will be conquered, and impurity will be eliminated from the air. Many persons will live in the healthy atmosphere of the building tops, while others will commute to far distant residential towns, or country homes.

Copyright Amazing Stories, 1939.

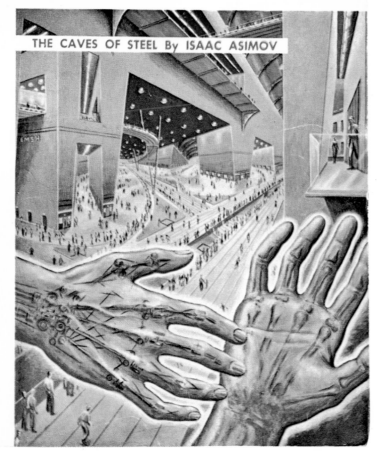

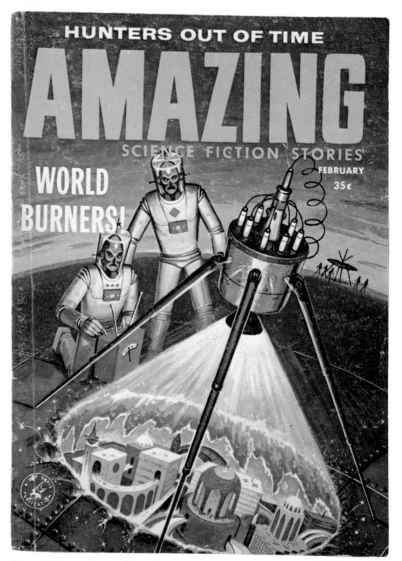

29. A cyclopean city with no human amenities. The vast proportions, together with lack of natural sky, combine to give an effect of vast size and claustrophobic closeness. A great place for walkers since there is no visible transport.

30. Ugly aliens burning a city of the future because they don't like its color scheme. Note unusual extra-terrestrial spark-plugs.

Facing page
28. **One of a series produced by** Amazing **magazine in 1949 on Cities of Tomorrow.**

33. Cave city at Bamiyan in Afghanistan. Despite impressive landscaping and clever use of natural geographic features, this city leaves much to be desired in daily amenities.

Above left
31. The fluid and menacing lines of space city Gail from the pen of Druillet, French illustrator and visionary.

Below left
32. An experimental design of the reconstruction and long range development of the Ilyich Square in Moscow, which gives the uncanny sensation of having been copied from a movie set.

Facing page, below
34. The day of judgment? Or perhaps the city is burning due to insufficient insulation around the power outlets. Logan's Run.

Above
35. A view of the City of Chaux, 1773.

In 1773 Nicolas Ledoux, architect to Louis XV, was comissioned to build a salt factory. He created a whole model city to be built around the factory, but only a small part of this great work was completed.

Facing page above
36. The Cannon Foundry, Chaux. Ledoux was attracted by the simple beauty of the pyramid.

Middle left
37. The Cemetery. Even the dead of Chaux had a grandiose labyrinth designed for them : only the top of the sphere was to be visible above the ground.

Middle right
38. Cooper's Workshop. 'Don't you know that an idea even quite bizarre can contain the germ of an excellent new conception?'

Below left
39. Woodcutter's House and Workshop – the lines of the pyramid again.

Below right
40. Quarters for Rural Caretakers, designed for the chateau of the Marquis de Montesquiou.

Next in our examination of unpleasant futuropoli is the possibility that we will be taken over by aliens. This has been the subject of much fiction and even more so-called fact. Great numbers of people believe that flying saucer people visit us daily to see how we are getting on, and have been doing so since before the beginning of recorded history. Obviously, aliens who can visit us when they like and still keep the best minds in the United States Air Force in doubt as to their very existence are capable of taking us over when they please. The fact that they have not done so yet can be interpreted in various ways. One possibility is that they are waiting until there are enough of us to be worth taking over. A work force of ten thousand million semi-intelligent beings (a figure attainable in less than thirty years) might be worth having even by galactic standards. The time may yet come when our worst fears are realized and the aliens come down in their ships and force us all to wear unbecoming gray uniforms and live in stainless steel and glass cities resembling chicken-growing stations.

Nor can we exclude the possibility of rule by the gods themselves. As used in science fiction today, the term 'god' has no religious significance. The gods of science-fiction are men and women of great longevity, incapable of being killed by ordinary means, and possessing superhuman powers of creation and destruction. They can be studied in many novels of Roger Zelazney and Phillip Jose Farmer. The cities ruled by these immortals are visually striking places, good places to live if you keep your nose out of the deity's business. Men and gods seem to get along better than just men alone : how else to account for the many legends of a golden age before history began, when men and gods lived together amicably ? How else to account for our present difficulties, now that the gods have gone away ?

Following possibilities opened up by Pavlov, and developed further by B. F. Skinner and others, we find that men can be motivated and controlled by the techniques of operant conditioning, better known as brainwashing. You could be conditioned to love your city whether you liked it or not. Even your activities within the city could be directed with complete certainty. Homing-type instincts could be implanted, making it unbearable for you to go away from Dearborn, or Leeds, or Brussels, or wherever you happened to be when they caught you and put you under the conditioning machine. They could make you want a holiday when it suited them, and make you want to go to a city-approved resort instead of wasting good money on going abroad. In this case, it wouldn't matter what Futuropolis was like: you would love it anyhow.

42. An American school of the future. Each tower contains a discipline – economy, science and culture.

43. One of the vertical-spatial variants of the organization of a Russian public centre, the basis of a community with a population of up to 150,000.

Facing page
41. **Illustration by Tony Roberts for** The City Dwellers.

Facing page
44. The Arrival **by Cliff McReynolds. (detail)**

45. The City Crumbles, **by Bob Layzell.**

A final and most unusual sort of Hell City is pictured by Brian Aldiss in his novel, Hothouse. Aldiss's Hell City is a single gigantic tree. In this story of the far future, there are no man-made constructions left on the face of the Earth. The sun is going nova, a gigantic banyon tree covers half the Earth, and a degenerate mankind lives in its branches and fights losing battles with mutated insects and vegetables. It is a striking vision, a rebuttal to Rousseau, and a reminder that no matter how bad our cities are, life is even worse without them.

46. Tier 3000 seems to be the perfect community of the future, with all the luxuries and amenities man could desire. But it is a suicidal and malignant paradise, threatening to turn into hell.

47. These weird fungoid growth are vast cylindrical towers forming 'trees' on which the individual dwellings come and go according to the natural time scale of their own proper 'metabolism'. Kiyonoru Kikutake, 1962.

48, 49. Fantastic and frightening cities from Urm le fou, by Philippe Druillet.

50. Artist's conception of the interior of the outer ring of the Island Three space colony designed by NASA. Mirrors at the top reflect light inside, and baffles prevent cosmic rays from entering. On the top deck is a typical housing complex. Housing is modular, permitting a variety of spaces and form-clusters. There will also be some open space for parks. Also visible is a track that will be part of a transit system. The second deck houses a service area that will provide storage, power distribution, and some processing equipment for light industry. Illustration by Donald Davis.

'Either you're part of the problem or you are part of the solution.'

Eldridge Cleaver

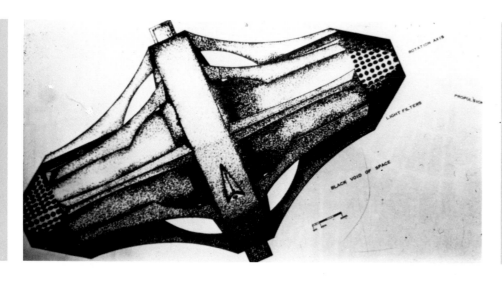

52. Asteromo, Paolo Soleri's design for a space city 2,600 metres long with an internal surface of 466 acres, supporting a population of 70,000.

Given the present situation on Earth, and the projections of current trends into the next century, it seems that most futuropoli on the drawing boards today are part of the problem.

The present world population is just over four and a half thousand million people. The UN's most optimistic forecast projects a world population of six and a half thousand million by the year 2000, eight and a half thousand million by 2020, 10 thousand million by 2035.

There are only two real alternatives. Either we go along as we are now, or we try something new.

To do something really new, we must take our planning beyond the Earth itself. Our planet is too small for us. Our sheer numbers and the magnitude of our problems force us to overuse and abuse the Earth. We are caught in a spiralling trap of increasing severity. It can be solved only by changing the frame of reference. We must move out into space.

Facing page
51. The interior could be made to resemble the Rocky Mountains or the Amazonian rain-forest. Earth-like gravity would be produced by centrifugal force of rotation of the large cylinder around its long axis. Sunlight coming through the glass 'windows' would be controlled to simulate day, night and changing seasons.

Facing page
53. 'No thunder thrills her peace, no sword of lightning scourges
These dim dark depths where lost Atlantis sleeps.'
Illustration by Joe Petagno.

54. Atlantis, looking very much like New York as seen from the harbor, being sunk by disgruntled city planners.

55. Pilkington's Sea City, projected to relieve the overcrowding of our land masses.

'Up to now, we have taken it for granted that huge cities were an inevitable part of industrialization. But what if it were possible to arrange an environment in which agricultural products could be grown with high efficiency, anywhere, at all times of the year? In which energy would be universally available, in unlimited quantities, at all times? In which transport would be as easy and cheap as ocean freight, not just to particular points, but to everywhere? There is, now, a possibility of designing such an environment . . .'

Gerald K. O'Neill, The High Frontier, p 42.

The colonization of space is not a visionary proposition. The technology is in existence, and the costs, though high, are not catastrophic. We could build a city in space right now. If we began today, it could be ready for occupation within a decade.

I am summarizing here some of the conclusions of Gerard K. O'Neill, taken from his book, The High Frontier: Human Colonies in Space. Dr O'Neill's work is so important that it deserves a chapter to itself.

Dr O'Neill is a physicist whose main research area is high-energy particle physics. How he came to the planning of future colonies is a story in itself, and well worth the reading. Here we will be able to examine only his proposal.

Initially, O'Neill's plan calls for a minimum-size space community just large enough to form a strong industrial base and thus be able to repay the cost of its construction. This would be Island One. It would be designed to be of economic value to Earth, converting solar energy to electricity and beaming it to microwave stations on Earth. It would also be capable of seeding more colonies like itself.

56. A futuristic city in space, looking not unlike New York in the thirties.

57. Titan City, capital of the Rootha Empire of Saturnia, visited by Dan Dare, Pilot of the Future on Operation Saturn, from the pages of Eagle, a boys' paper of the fifties.

Island One will be an artificial spherical world in space. It will have a circumference of nearly a mile, and will rotate at 1.97 rotations per minute, providing Earth-normal gravity. The settlements and living areas of Island One will be spread on the inner walls of the pressurized sphere, extending halfway up from the 'equator'. At this level, gravity will be reduced to seventy percent of Earth-normal, and will set out the present limits of the habitat.

Sunlight will enter the sphere with the aid of planar mirrors positioned outside of windows set into the upper levels of the sphere. An ideal climate can be arranged for the Island if only agreement can be reached on what constitutes ideal climate.

The circumference of the sphere at its equator will be a good place to locate a river, with shoreline beaches set alongside, and perhaps with picnic sites, little lakes for bathing and boating, and with restaurants and rustic taverns, as desired.

A zero-gravity corridor will extend through the sphere, providing ventilation, heat exchange, and quick transport to the surface.

Above
58. Future generations may re-create cities of the Earth on their new planets as giant museums in honour of their forebears.

Right
59. Spaceship City, a gigantic wheel 50 metres in diameter, with the crew members asleep from birth to death in individual cabins, awakening only when the Spaceship reaches the Promised Land, where they will found a new Babylon . . . or New York . . . or Moscow. Superstudio.

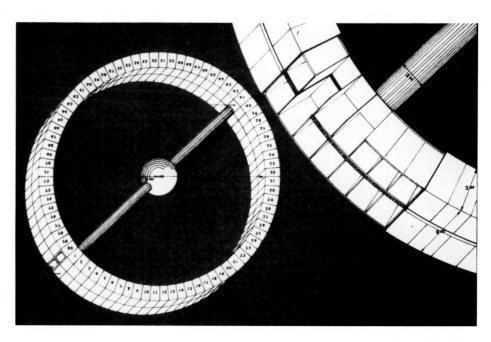

Domes are a recurring feature of future cities – perhaps because they imply a controlled atmosphere that a humanoid may safely breathe.

60. French artist Moebius has integrated domes into this science fiction city.

61. Arcosanti, a future city designed by Paolo Soleri around spheres and semispheres to accommodate 15,000 people, and built over seven acres.

62. A hemidome two miles in diameter to enclose Manhattan, conceived by Buckminster Fuller.

64. Extraterrestrial transportation center, by Robert McCall. The journey to the planets begins here. Supersonic shuttles bring in passengers from all over Earth.

Facing page
63. **Angus McKie's illustration for** Green Hills of Earth.

65. A bird's eye view of a huge city built inside the crater of a remote planet – back-packing takes on a new meaning.

Island One would have impressive amenities. Low gravity swimming pools could be located high up near the rotational axis of this corridor. In this area of reduced gravity, it would also be possible to fly pedal-operated airplanes as easily and safely as one rows a boat on Earth.

Island One is designed for a population of 10,000. A desirable plan might be to separate the usable land area of the sphere into three 'villages', each of just over 3,000 people. Many types of living community could be built on this land area. Dr O'Neill presents an attractive plan:

'I would have a preference, I think, for one rather appealing arrangement: to leave the valleys free for small villages, forests, and parks; to have lakes in the valley ends, at the foot of the mountains, and to have small cities rising into the foothills from the lake shores. Even at the high-population density that might characterize a nearly habitat, that arrangement would seem rather pleasant: a house in a small village where life could be relaxed and children could be raised with room to play; and just five or ten miles away, a small city . . .'

O'Neill, The High Frontier.

The inhabitants of Island One would have 4.5 square meters of personal living space—probably better than most of them could do on Earth. It would be a gracious life, though you might get sick of the parties after a while.

Island One is designed to be self-supporting. Agriculture will be centralized in a separate external container attached to Island One. Here intensive year-round agriculture will be carried out on an automated basis in a climate that can be adjusted precisely. Smaller livestock could also be accommodated, though the importation of herds of cattle will have to wait for the development of larger Islands.

Industry for Island One will similarly be located outside the habitat but nearby, in its own cylinder. The colony's first task might well be the transmission of electrical power to Earth. Located in space in continual strong sunshine, Island One will be able to convert light to electricity by existing technology. With the growth of further Islands, the amount of energy that can be produced in space could satisfy all of Earth's needs.

66. Simplicity itself – a radial piece of town planning conceived in sixteenth century Italy.

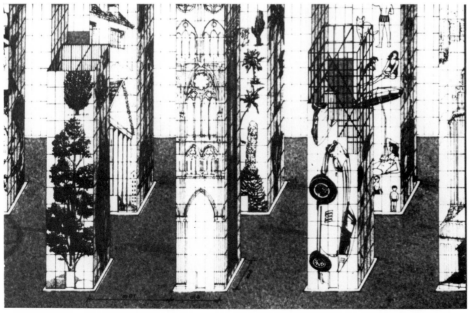

67. City of the Splendid Houses, in which each citizen's goal is the possession of the most beautiful house, to which end they spend all their leisure hours and spare wage coupons in decoration and embellishment.

Right

68. Island Three agricultural area. On the top four levels soybeans, wheat, sorghum and some other crops would be grown. Bottom level is a drying facility. The fish tanks could hold some 260,000 fish and the half-mile farm could also house 2,800 cattle. Three of these farms, covering 110 acres, could produce enough food to make the space colony self-sufficient.

This would be a modest beginning. More ambitious is Island Three, which Dr O'Neill describes as a medium size project. Its basic design would consist of a coupled pair of cylinders twenty miles long and four miles in diameter. The habitat cylinder would have a total land area of 500 square miles, half of which could be used for living space and recreation. Island Three could comfortably house four million people and thus would be a sort of continent in space upon which many cities would be built. Without much difficulty it could feed a population of ten million.

Places such as these Islands would be capable of sustaining large populations. They could be used to siphon off excess populations of existing countries on Earth. Space shuttle services from all the continents could bring people to their new homes at a tolerable cost.

Dr O'Neill points out that a rich source of minerals and chemicals of all kinds lies in the asteroid belt. They could be reached from the Islands with modest expenditure of energy. Slow-moving space tugs, with crews of six or eight and good film libraries, would sail the lonely spaces between the Islands and the asteroids. Extensive mining and refining operations would be carried out there. Habitats would be built in the asteroid belt, restaurants and shopping centers would spring up next, and industrial civilization would spread. A population of unlimited numbers could be self-supporting out there.

THE VISUAL ENCYCLOPEDIA OF SCIENCE FICTION

A DOCUMENTED PICTORIAL CHECKLIST OF THE SF WORLD-CONCEPTS/THEMES/BOOKS/MAGS/COMICS/FILMS/TV/RADIO/ART/FANDOM/CULTS/PERSONAL COMMENTARIES BY THE GREATEST NAMES IN SF WRITING... EDITED BY BRIAN ASH

70. Alphabet cities, that could be to the future what sky-writing is to the present. Illustration by Tim White

Facing page
69. Artist's conception of the Island Three space colony, designed by NASA. Several hundred thousand people could live here, with California-style amenities. A good place to bring up your children.

71. The Bridge over the Stars, kingdom of Torquedara Varenkor, creation of Philippe Druillet.

Facing page
72. The giant astroport of Delirius, planet devoted to the gratification of pleasure in any shape or form. Philippe Druillet.

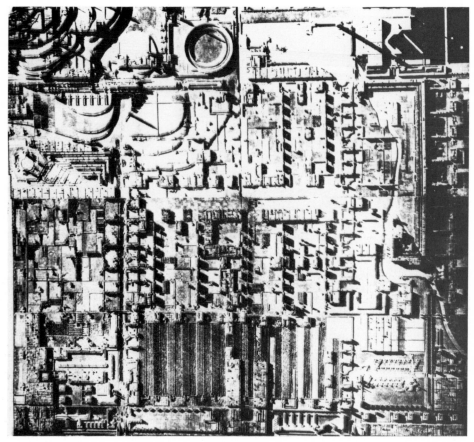

Above
73. Frank Lloyd Wright's 1932 design for a decentralised city – Broadacre.

Above
74. Another creation of bizarre cityscape by the French artist Moebius.

Below
75. Le Corbusier's City of Towers, a project for 60-storey apartment blocks amidst gardens and playingfields, the kind of high-rise development now regarded as one of the social disasters of twentieth century town planning.

Facing page
76. Illustration by George Underwood.

More visions of ideal cities, the supreme achievement of twenty thousand years of civilization, from the fertile brains of Superstudio.

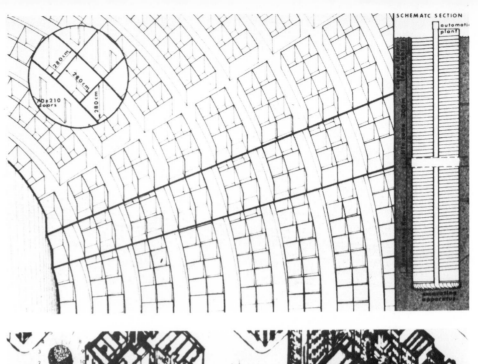

77. Temporal Cochlea-city, an endless screw 4.5 km in diameter, completing one revolution a year. Its propulsion apparatus is an atomic power center set to last 10,000 years. The living-cells are arranged in a double row of concentric circles.

78. City of Order – where the inhabitants are programmed to fit the city, so that no one complains about the unpunctuality of the buses, or ever parks on a double yellow line.

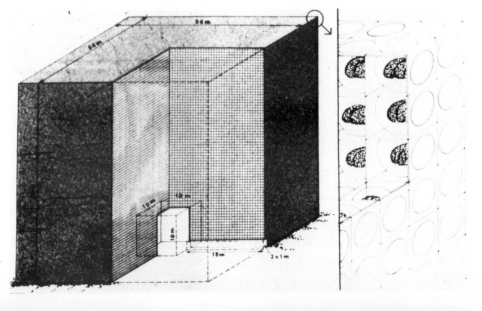

79. New York of Brains. In the charred space that was New York, stands a cube filled with 10″ cubic containers in each of which floats a brain. Completely cut off from external perception, they are free to reach the supreme goals of wisdom and madness – perhaps to reach absolute knowledge.

80. Conical Terraced City. Living in 500 circular terraces one above the other with no connecting stairways, the city's inhabitants receive orders and thought programmes from above. Their one goal is to lighten the burden of orders filtering down by somehow clambering upwards, eventually to reach the one-man cupola at the top.

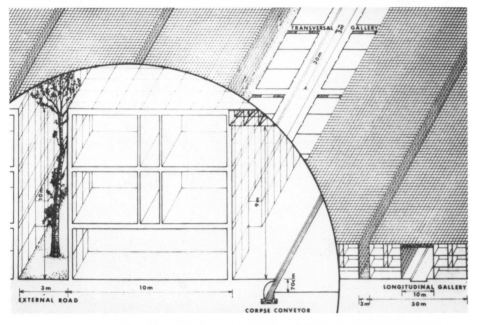

81. City of the Book. The book that all citizens live by is the spirit of the city. Left-hand pages (ethics) can be read only by outside light from the external road, and right-hand pages (behavior) only in the dark, created by the longitudinal tunnels. Since the regulations governing behavior are the result of behavioral tendencies in Western cultures freed from moralistic overtones, most citizens choose to live in the dark.

82. The Thirteenth City. It was known that an ideal form of society and life had been developed in the thirteenth city. But its form and dimensions are indefinite and unknowable, the blueprints unavailable for consultation.

83. The extravagant grand temple of Druillet's
Delirius, and if you don't come and pay homage
immediately . . .

84. Robert McCall's space colony in the form of a gigantic wheel. Centrifugal force produces simulated gravity at the rim, reducing to zero gravity at the hub.

85. A spherical pneumatic structure devised by Frei Otto to make possible ordinary living and working conditions in the Arctic or any unfavorable climate, by means of a pre-assembled inflatable skin in a cable net.

Right and facing page
86, 87. The Atlantis myth has always been a fertile source for fiction writers and film makers. Here is a film set reconstruction of the lost city by MGM in 1961, while opposite is a thirties version of a modern Atlantis, whose various levels contain a golf course, tennis courts and a palm garden.

Dr O'Neill is a highly respected scientist. He has worked on these plans with many top-level scientists. Carl Sagan, himself a highly respected authority on man's possibilities in space has said:

'Our technology is capable of extraordinary new ventures in space, one of which is the space city idea which Gerard O'Neill has described. That's an extremely expensive undertaking, but it seems to me historically of the greatest significance. The engineering aspects of it as far as I can tell are perfectly well worked out by O'Neill's study group. It is practical.'

Having said all this, one must point out some of the difficulties that are likely to be encountered in this proposal. It seems to me that the main problem would be psychological. As an exercise in pure engineering, the Islands could undoubtably be made to work. As a social experiment, we would expect small groups of carefully chosen scientists, engineers, and technicians to perform well in this environment, just as they do in the Antarctic.

However—dedicated scientists can be expected to live successfully in any imaginable environment: the tougher it is, the more motivated they are to carry it through well. This could not be expected of a population at large, for whom these cities in space must be intended if they are to be relevant to our problems on Earth. It might be difficult or impossible for a non-scientist to consider a little floating metal ball as a true home. No matter how prettily it is embellished with low-gravity swimming pools, artificial beaches man-made mountains and the like, one would still be continually aware of how thin, artificial and restricted one's environment really was.

Unless the space cities can provide meaningful and absorbing activities for the multitudes who will occupy them, boredom and dissatisfaction will be inevitable. These problems are unlikely to be satisfied by the many hobbies and cultural pursuits that the futuropoli in space can be expected to provide. Daily life might be very much like life on a luxury liner—pleasant for a week or two but unsatisfactory for much longer.

Two popular science fiction novels starring extra-ordinary cities.

Right
89. A 1954 edition of City at World's End.

Below
88. 1974 cover design for Cities in Flight, picturing one of the cities that has broken loose from Earth.

90. On the River, a Superstudio design recalling the Great Wall of China or the magnificent Roman aqueducts.

91. Multi-purpose hall at the Federal Garden Exhibition 1975, Mannheim, designed by Frei Otto and others.

Overleaf
92. The Martian Base by Leslie Carr, based on a drawing by R A Smith.

There will not be much possibility of real change and variety. If you don't happen to be much interested in exploring the asteroid belt, you will have difficulties in finding anywhere to go for a change of pace. Taking a holiday back on Earth would be prohibitively expensive. The only places you could go would be to some neighboring space stations or possibly the Moon base. You would find a similar artificial environment in all these places. Your life would be like a supporting role in a NASA film.

Entertaining the populations of the space stations will probably be a greater problem than feeding and housing them. To this end, special-purpose amusement worlds in space might well be built. These would provide pleasure facilities, perhaps in the forms of bars, amusement parks, pornography centers.

These entertainment worlds would be self-supporting, as entertainment always is. They would provide a place for disaffected Earth people, with artistic leanings, and might ultimately prove more valuable than the industrial installations.

The very perfection of the space station would make it a dull place to live in. A perfect climate sounds nice but can be very boring on a year around basis. People seem to need a certain degree of change and variety every day. It is difficult to simulate this.

93. It's alarming but not surprising how often an earlier generation's science fiction is now turning into reality. 'Giant, bird-like atoplanes filled the air, carrying on much of the world's travel and commerce. Many buildings had flat-topped structures affording landing stages.'

The MOON OF DOOM by Earl L. Bell

Facing page above
94. Another of Robert McCall's visions of a city of tomorrow, Solar.

Below
95. The space city is on the left. On the right, lying in a vast plain, is the guts of the operation, a solar field that converts sunlight into micro-waves and transmits the energy to stations on Earth. One-man work modules on the right repair meteor damage to the solar field. Illustration by Robert McCall.

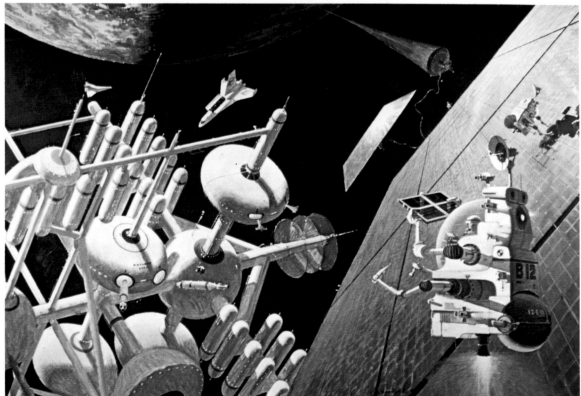

The Islands in space are an exciting and important proposal. By all present indications, they will become increasingly necessary in the next century. The social and psychological problems will have to be solved. Until they are, it is difficult to see this as a satisfactory way of life for large numbers of ordinary people. Without the frontier mentality of dedication and willingness to work for an ideal larger than immediate gratification, the Islands might be suitable only for visionaries, refugees and prisoners. Environmental diversification is urgently needed. A great deal of work will be required on this aspect of the problem.

96, 97. Creations of the present for recreations of the future? A project for turning desolate waste land near Nuneaton, England, into Civilia, a leisure and holiday centre.

98. A scene from Osaka Expo 70 showing RK and RM robots by Arata Isosaki.

99. Arcube, a future city with a population of 400,000, 1,500 meters high and covering 346 acres. Another of Paolo Soleri's projects in high-density construction.

100. The kingdom of Céméroon, created by Druillet. Built of basalt, porphyry and marble, of meteors and fire.

101. This city has a frantically busy design, possibly inspired by roller coaster architecture. The man in the foreground is scanning the horizon for signs of life.

Facing page
102. An alien city designed to over-awe. The bumble bee men in the foreground are discussing where to locate the new Center for the Performing Arts.

GOLDEN CITY ON TITAN Orro, greatest city of the solar system's largest moon, is a city of skyscrapers that equal those of Earth. Its people are highly intelligent and civilized. (Details on page 145)

103. Instant City Airships, a travelling Ideas
Circus dreamt up by Peter Cook of Archigram.

'Going all basic and back to first principles you reach stage three: the only real difference between a house and the clothing you wear is one of size—your clothes form a one-man skin and your house will allow any number of people in it. Both are subject to changes of fashion and both cover up to differing extents one's indecencies—but it's interesting to compare how the skins that form the enclosures of the house are traditionally permanent while the clothing skins are removable/replacable to suit any whim of climate, sexual fetish or what-have-you. But in principle an overcoat is a house/is a car when a motor's clipped on.'

Michael Webb and David Green, Archigram, p 55.

'More and more people want to determine their own parameters of behavior. They want to decide how they shall behave, whether it's playing, working, loving, etc. People are less and less prepared to accept imposed rules and patterns of behavior. Doing your own thing is important.

'People are becoming more interested in people and reality, rather than in feeding mythical systems.

'Unfortunately, however, in terms of doing your own thing, architecture is clearly not working.'

Webb and Green, Archigram, p 112.

Many peoples of the ancient world have carried their cities with them. American Indians, Tartars, Mongols, Turks, Huns, Bedouin; all have been nomadic city dwellers.

When a Roman legion was on the march, it stopped and built a city every night complete with palisade, and ditch, and red-light district for the camp followers. Greek armies did the same, although the streets were not as straight. When the Germanic tribes were migrating into Europe, their homes were the large wooden carts they travelled in. They converted them into dwellings when they wanted to stay for a while, packed them up when they wanted to move. These carts—one-family vehicle/homes—were powered by interchangeable energy units called oxen.

104.   10,000 Years Hence. A Prediction. A moving city visualized in 1922. Designed to float several miles above the surface of the Earth. 'Four gigantic generators will shoot earthward electric rays which will produce the force to keep the city aloft'. The city was to be roofed over, and would derive its power from the sun, converting solar into electrical energy.

Right
106. Transportation center floating in the sky. Given the development of anti-gravity devices, this is an entirely feasible plan. Illustration by Robert McCall.

Below
105. An extremely mobile city this one, but does the air-traffic controller know his job?

These themes of movability and mutability have provided a powerful metaphor for the Archigram Group, a loose collection of architects and city-planners who introduced many exciting ideas in the 60s and 70s.

Archigram has taken inspiration from space technology, particularly from Cape Kennedy, where the archetype of Archigram's Walking City exists. Other influences have been Disneyland, where the fun city of the future is alive and well in the present; science fiction; and pop culture in general.

They are into easily conformable spaces—adaptable multi-purpose rooms within an adaptable milieu. The emphasis is on flow and change. To get with it you must be willing to embrace the new and unprecedented. If you really want to look out your window at old church steeples, Archigram will be happy to provide you with a holographic scene setter.

They have moved away from the traditional concept of a city as a fixed collection of dirty masonry filled with dour-faced factory workers. Archigram's work tries to explore the very meaning of a city. They have come up with many provocative ways of putting people together.

Archigram is into interchangeable building units, perhaps to be manufactured on the city site itself. They have designed Plug-In-City—detachable and exchangeable units grouped around a transportation grid, capable of easy adaptability for changing demands. They have proposals for Instant Cities, to be set up in open areas with the elan of a rock festival. Their concepts are joyous, and they might even be technologically possible.

The inevitable critique of Archigram is aesthetic. Cities you can put together and take apart at will are unlikely to satisfy one's need for beauty and stability in one's surroundings, or to add much to the advancement of the arts. Still, it is an engaging vision, as the following scenario tries to demonstrate.

'The Cushicle is an invention that enables a man to carry a complete environment on his back. It inflates-out when needed. It is a complete nomadic unit—and it is fully serviced.'

107. Instant City project by Stanley Tigerman, 1968. An abstract, tetrahedral design, the structure beautifully worked out – 'but where do you sleep and where do you dine?'

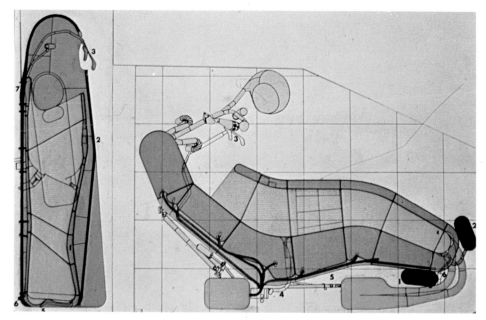

108, 109.   The Cushicle is an invention that enables a man to carry a complete environment on his back. It inflates out when needed. It is a complete nomadic unit, and it is fully serviced. The Cushicle carries food, water supply, radio, miniature projection television and heating apparatus.

It has two main constituent parts, the 'armature' or 'spinal' system which forms the chassis and support for the appliances and other apparatus. The other is the enclosure part which is basically an inflated envelope with extra skins as viewing screens. Both systems open out consecutively or can be used independently.

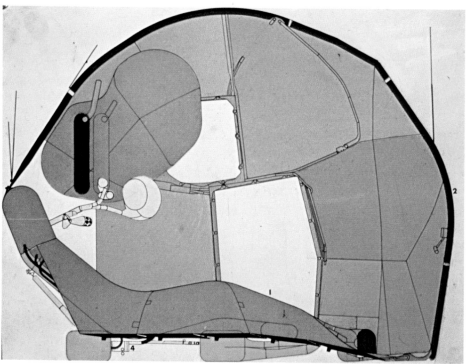

'Clothing for living in—or if it wasn't for my Suitaloon I would have to buy a house.'

One-man or one-family vehicle/dwelling units would make up Nomad City. The units would be individually self-sufficient. They would expand to make a house, reduce to become an automobile, or collapse to the size of a suitcase for storage. Every unmarried adult or head of family would be issued one. The City would be composed entirely of these transport/habitat units, though some provision might have to be made for a separate City Hall, post office, and jail.

In Nomad City, many different geometries could be applied to the three-dimensional ordering of the unit components. Changes in the shape or appearance of the City could be made as often as desired. National contests might well be run for Cleverest City of the Month.

Individual unit owners in Nomad City would come and go as they pleased, after they had given twenty-four hours notice so that another unit could be plugged into their place in the City structure. From time to time the entire City might move to another physical situation; when the old one became boring, for example.

In the summer, we might expect Nomad City to be reduced by perhaps a fourth of its usual size and population as inhabitants leave notes for the milkman, shut off the power, detach from the position, and drive away in their car/home for three weeks in the Med or Miami Beach, possibly joining up with friends and neighbors from back home in a holiday grid on the shores of Biscayne Bay or just off St Tropez.

Nomad Cities would probably travel a lot, and there might be some difficulty in locating them. A self-updating computerized A-Z City Finder would be needed. You would consult it to learn where the city of your choice was presently located, and for how long, and then you would phone ahead to reserve a plug-in site close to the theater district. There might have to be a central locating service for lost or strayed cities, however.

110. Flying fortresses of doom and destruction, as illustrated in a 1931 science fiction story The Spacehounds of IPC.

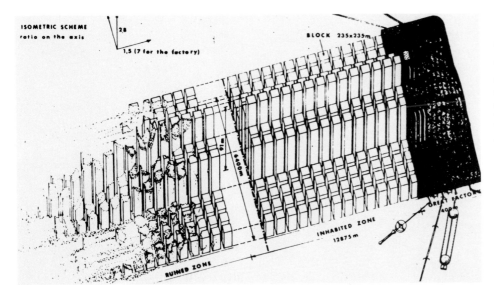

111. Continuous production conveyor belt city, which moves unrolling like a majestic serpent, over new lands, taking its 8 million inhabitants on a ride through valleys and hills, from the mountains to the seashore, generation after generation. It is headed by the Grand Factory, which exploits the land and underground materials of the territory it crosses and from these extracts all it requires for the continuing construction of the city. Superstudio.

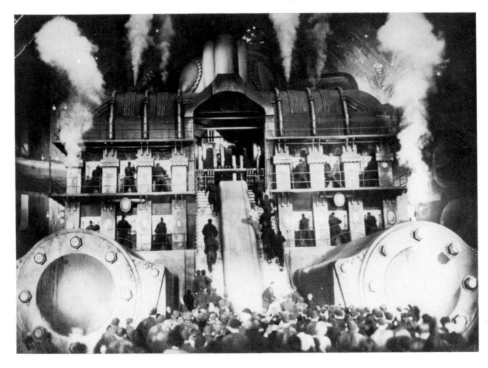

112. Another conveyor belt scene, but one much less benevolent. In Fritz Lang's classic film Metropolis, the machine demands a constant sacrifice of human souls and bodies.

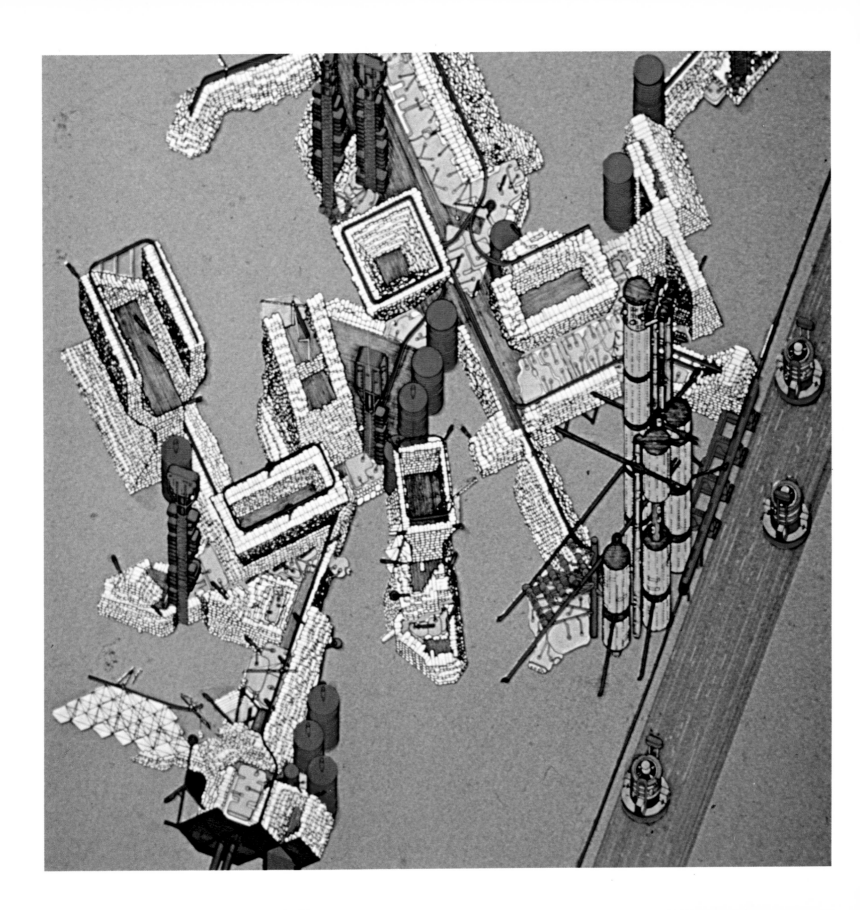

The theme of self-contained moving cities has been popular in science fiction. A recent use of it can be seen in Christopher Priest's Inverted World. The central image in this novel is of a city standing alone on a vast plain. The city has been constructed to move on rails. As the city advances rails are taken up from behind and put down in front. The city's ability to move isolates it from outside influence. Another variation on this theme can be seen in Robert Heinlein's novelette, Universe. In this fine story, a spaceship/city world is journeying endlessly between the stars. The inhabitants have long forgotten their destination, forgotten even that they are on a spaceship. They have reverted to savagery and are unaware of anything beyond their immediate environment.

Movement does not have to be isolating, however. In Jim Blish's Cities in Flight novels, there is plenty of interaction. Earth possesses an advanced space-age technology, but is caught in a severe economic depression. The invention of an interstellar propulsion unit called the spindizzy has made it possible for entire destitute cities to pull themselves off the bedrock and take off into space. Once in space, these nomad cities hire out their skills to other, more prosperous civilizations. Blish calls them 'Okie Cities', for they are the modern-day equivalent of the hoboes and other itinerant workers of the past.

Without a spindizzy, most moving cities may have to wait for better times, when a surplus of wealth and energy can go to their building, and a revitalized landscape be provided for their travels.

Facing page
113. **Plug-In City** – the romance of component compatibility. Like a great mechanized jigsaw puzzle, the city can be shaped to produce many diverse images. Archigram.

114. A 1974 cover design for James Blish's classic, the fourth and last volume of Cities in Flight, **originally entitled** The Triumph of Time.

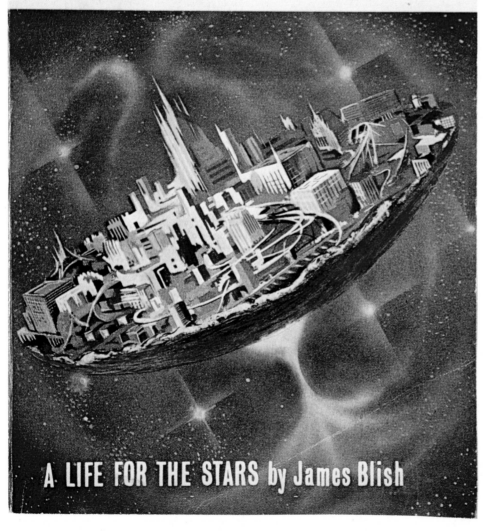

JANUARY 2'6

analog
SCIENCE FACT ⏦ SCIENCE FICTION

A LIFE FOR THE STARS by James Blish

116. A city travelling between the stars. The force-shield is not shown, but is undoubtedly there to protect the inhabitants from the biting solar winds.

Facing page
115. Illustration for Green Odyssey, by Angus McKie.

The nomadic principle of unit mobility and self-sufficiency can be adapted to many circumstances, however. The nomadic unit can provide an irreducible habitat under extreme conditions, and can serve as an exploration probe into new territory. We see these qualities exploited to the fullest in the following scenario.

The time is the near future. The unthinkable has happened—an atomic war has broken out between the great powers. Soviet and American retaliatory strikes are pressed to the utmost. It is a quick war and it results in the utter devastation of Western civilization.

117. The menacing cityscape of Fritz Lang's Metropolis.

Above ground, there is nothing but endless stretches of smoking wreckage and charred farmland. Grisly fires burn at night, and columns of smoke rise by day over the ruins of once-proud cities. Ninety-five percent of the population has been snuffed in the first week. The only survivors are scattered bands of disorganized hippies who engage in battles with monstrous mutated insects and venemous vegetables.

Luckily, some far-sighted men have been prepared for for just this eventuality. They are, of course, the very people who were in charge of things before the holocaust. With a little luck they will soon be in charge again.

In preparation for this day, Burrow Cities have been built beneath major cities in Europe and the United States. To avoid panic, and because of insufficient room, these cities are kept secret from the population at large, their construction disguised as new subway extensions. When the warning of attack comes especially selected industrialists, politicians, scientists, military men, and their advisors and dependents go down to the nearest Burrow. Here they wait, ready to rebuild civilization exactly as it has been before the holocaust, only this time without Communists.

Their Burrow Cities are not intended to be used in the conventional manner of cities, however. They are collection points, jump-off stages where the survivors will be issued the essential equipment and maps they need for exploring and colonizing underground.

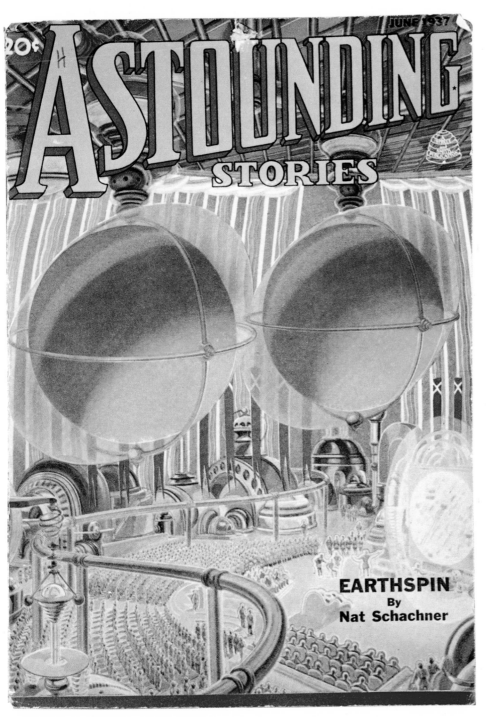

Above

119.   Project plan of Paris (architect Sauvage): the city is not conceived as a modern Babylon, but at any rate the individual is allotted the maximum of free healthy living space.

Left

118.   1937 conception of a future city. We see a man addressing a large assembly. He may be trying to explain the function of the enormous pink balloons – astounding!

The Burrow concept is built around a single new tool. Simple though it is that tool will reshape the course of human destiny. It is the one-family Mole, as developed from the Earth's Core novels of Edgar Rice Burroughs.

The Mole is a self-sufficient vehicle/home/environment. Individually or in packs, Moles can go exploring through the Earth's crust, and set up housekeeping in suitable areas—moist underground caverns, for example, where intensive mushroom farming can be practised.

Moles will derive their energy by converting the friction of their passage into electricity by a process that is still under development. Further energy sources could be developed by burrowing toward the Earth's molten core, where an inexhaustible source of radiant energy is waiting to be tapped.

When favorable sites are reached, Moles will assemble and plug into each other by way of gaskets, coming together to trade, or for parties and square dances. In time, true Burrow Cities may appear as special-purpose Molers set up as blacksmiths, cabinetmakers, etc. Other Molers will doubtless resist the urge to settle down in favor of the thrill of exploring the unknown universe of the Earth's crust.

The Mole is an important physical extension of the Western dream of individual freedom and initiative, translated into sub-Earth idiom. It will offer a hard frontier life, but it will be a rewarding one. There will be many problems to solve. Waste disposal, for example. One possible solution for this will be to bale up all the wastes and feed them into the exit tubes of live volcanoes, which will spit them out of sight onto the surface of the planet.

These wastes can always be shoveled back underground again if the surface should ever be reclaimed.

The Time Oscillator
by Henry F. Kirkham

120. Roll up and see the show! 'I saw a vast concourse of queerly dressed people. They were standing before a mighty revolving globe that scintillated with all the colors of the rainbow. Now and again they swayed back and forth.'

Cities are built in response to the technology of their times, or to exploit new technology. If we knew what the important inventions and processes of the future will be, we could know a great deal more about the shape and function of cities to come. No major breakthrough seems imminent in the physical sciences just now. But there is a potentially revolutionary situation going on in psychology and theoretical physics. This could have incalculable effects upon city-planning.

The development and control of extrasensory ability seems just around the corner. Courses will soon be available in clairvoyance and clairaudience. Upon graduation you will be able to dispense with telephones and communicate directly with people mind to mind. There is at present a place in California where you can receive instruction in the art of levitation, though with no guarantee of success.

Teleportation will undoubtedly be a key skill in the next development of consciousness. This ability, much written about in science fiction, will be your passport to a magical new world in which distance has been abolished. No longer will you need a car, train, boat or jet. Getting around will be simple: a few minutes of intense concentration, the intoning of a suitable mantra, and an instant later you will be at your destination, cool and collected, and with no parking problem.

This ability would confer enormous advantages on its possessor, giving him abilities that once were considered superhuman. So great would the teleporter's power be that we might expect the technique to be kept secret, given out only to initiates, veiled in secrecy and mystery for as long as possible.

A specialized elite might be expected to arise, a new class of men and women who have mastered extra-sensory skills. They would become the next rulers of mankind.

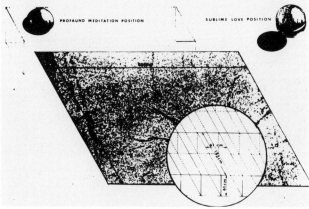

121. City of the Hemispheres. The flat shiny surface is made up of the covers of over 10 million crystal sarcophagi, each containing an immobile individual connected to a central bloodstream. A series of electrodes applied to the cranium control an external sensory apparatus, a free-moving hemisphere of silvery metal. Two hemispheres may unite in the position of sublime love – a spiritual union only, as there is no need to create life in a place where death does not exist. Superstudio.

122. Two moving cities from the adventures of
Flash Gordon, one hovering underwater and the
other fixed in space.

A situation like this is pictured in Fritz Leiber's fine science fiction novel, Gather, Darkness! The time is the future, We are in the impressive gothic city of Megatheopolis. From here, a religious hierarchy rules a world of superstitious peasants. The priests of the Great God have all sorts of powers supposedly derived from the deity himself. They have haloes and cloaks which act as protective devices, and they possess rods charged with 'spiritual' power. With these and other devices they overawe their subjects.

We soon learn, however, that the wands and haloes are straightforward technology decked out in supernatural disguise to impress the gullible. Leiber's religious hierarchy is made up of clever knaves imposing themselves on fools.

Gather, Darkness! was an appropriate extrapolation when science-fiction (in imitation of science itself) was trying to maintain a firm boundary between scientific rationalism and mystical nonsense. All effects, no matter how apparently inexplicable, had to have a rational basis. But today the situation is different. Written today, it would be scientifically respectable for Leiber's religious hierarchy to be manifesting powers of mind rather than of technology.

With government in the hands of a class of psi technicians, we can expect to see some stunning architecture. The cyclopean style must come naturally when you can levitate enormous blocks of marble as if they were bricks. There are claims that this is how Tiryns, Mycenae, Tenochtitlan, and other great cities of the past were built. Perhaps we will see their like again.

Cities built by mysterious supermen tend to have short lifespans. Their purported histories tell much the same story over and over again: how a group of people somehow develop heightened mental abilities, produce a mighty civilization, and then are swallowed up by earthquake or flood, and their secret lost. Undoubtedly it was easier to lose important things in the past, when there were no communications, natural calamities were more frequent, and the population small and scattered. This time we might be luckier, avoiding destruction long enough for the secret to filter down to the general population. Then, at last, the Faustian dream will be realized and every man can be a magician. The Psionic Age will have begun.

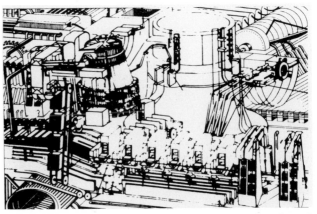

123. Ninth City – the city as a machine, so large that not even its inhabitants know its size. They travel along obligatory routes, finding food and fear, sleep and joy, sex and hope, death and anger, sometimes also rebellion, but they know that if they get off their programmed route, they will inevitably be crushed by the machinery which rules them. Superstudio.

Right
124.   An Okie city, either taking off or landing. In either case, the Indian in the foreground is going to have quite a story to tell back at the tepee.

Below
125.   Crater City design by Archigram. Vertical cave dwellings for the troglodytes of the future as the wheel of history turns full circle.

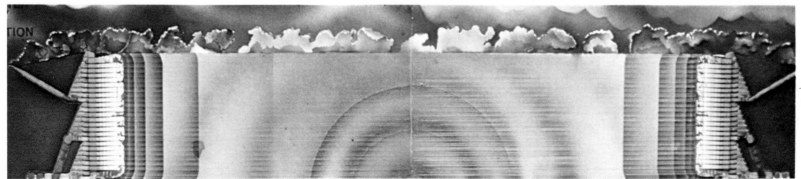

A CITY ON PLUTO

Profundo, sub-surface city of the Bat-Men of Pluto. Here on this icy, distant world, the only place for a city is underground. It is an amazing world of cavern-cities, bat-like men, and greatly advanced science. (See page 146 for complete details)

126.   Amazing **back cover**, 1941.

127.   Le Corbusier's Ville Contemporaine.

128. Construction for a Modern Metropolis by Mario Chiattone, one of the Italian Futurists of the early twentieth century, which has the feeling of an elaborate stage set – life here might be a sterile existence.

In the Psionic Age, people will require very different cities from anything they have today. Our current cities must be concentrated and dense in order to allow us to get from home to work and back again without taking all day at it. Sometimes it takes all day anyhow. But the Psionic Age will change all that. Gone will be the traffic jams and railroad strikes of the past. There will be no cars to jam or trains to strike. The streets will be clean and quiet, and you will be able to teleport from your home in New York to Joe's Stone Crab Restaurant in Miami Beach easier (and in greater safety) than if you were to walk around the corner to your local Chinese restaurant. Nor is that all. You will be able to teleport to London for the January sales, to Bangkok to buy your furniture, to Ireland to do your grocery shopping, and to Tierra del Fuego for an unusual low cost holiday.

The entire Earth would thus become a single city with its surround. Teleportation would encourage a Distanced style of life. You might have your kitchen in France, your bedroom in Sweden, your garden in Italy, and your bathroom in America; or any other arrangement you choose. Each person's city would be unique, a conceptual city made up of the bits of the Earth that he wanted to spend time in.

It would certainly be a good life. But a problem arises as to who is to pay for it all. The teleporters can't be expected to; not when evasion is so simple. No customs could keep track of a population of telepaths, no police could restrict them, no walls could keep them in or out. For better or worse we would be free, and answerable only to ourselves. Perhaps we could devise completely automatic routines to maintain our cities, grow the crops and manufacture the goods. Then mankind would be left with nothing to do but try to figure out what to do next.

Facing page
129. There was a Crooked House **by Alan Daniels.**

Walt Disney World lies just southwest of Orlando, Florida. It comprises some 27,000 acres, or roughly twice the size of Manhattan. Nearly a third of this land—7500 acres—is devoted to a wilderness conservation plan. In the other 20,000 acres, we find the world-famous entertainment complex called The Magic Kingdom. This is what most people think of when they think of Walt Disney World. But the Magic Kingdom takes up only 100 acres. In addition to it, Walt Disney World has a residential community called Buena Vista, an industrial park, a large entrance complex with hotels and parking facilities, and a STOL jetport. Projected for 1981, there will also be EPCOT—'Experimental Prototype Community for Tomorrow'.

The magic Kingdom is the heart of the operation and its raison d'être. It is divided into six regions—Fantasyland, Tomorrowland, Main Street, Liberty Square, Adventureland, and Frontierland. They are tied together by an ultra-modern monorail system, and supported by other forms of non-polluting transport.

Hidden out of sight below the Magic Kingdom, there is an entire city invisible to the public. Down here are the controls and services for the elaborate operations above. Here the food is cooked, garbage is collected by another ultra-modern system and compacted, repairs are carried out, etc. The people who work down here are never seen by the public. Their endeavors are guided by yet another ultra-modern computer system. Everything in Disney World is ultra-modern, the most advanced of its kind.

The Magic Kingdom is a circular array of village-sized regions connected by monorail and foot routes. The various regions are independent of each other, physically separated except for specific routes. Each region presents architectural and theatrical variations on a single fantasy theme. The regions are self-consistent, but have little but a stylistic relationship to each other. The buildings within The Magic Kingdom, like Cinderella's Castle or The Crystal Palace, are cute and ingratiating, scaled down to seven-eighths lifesize and boldly colored and modelled. For the millions who come here each year, it is a place of inexhaustible delights.

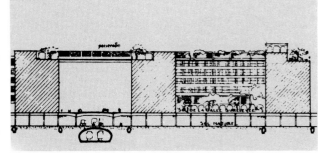

131. An early (1915) Corbusier design for a town built on piles which serve as foundations for the houses. The actual 'ground' of the town is a sort of floor, beneath which all the main services are directly accessible.

Facing page
130. Multi-level city. The sphere and pyramid motif break up the squareness of the city, while the leaning pyramid provides a classical echo in an otherwise modern scheme. Designed by Ean Taylor.

Above
132.   Here is Disneyworld's A-frame hotel. The monorail takes us quickly into the wonders of the Magic Kingdom.
Photograph © Walt Disney Productions.

Right
133.   **The futuristic setting of** Logan's Run.

Facing page
134.   **Cinderella's Castle in the Magic Kingdom.** Eighteen storeys high, completely air-conditioned with glass mosaic murals in the shape of Gothick arches. Elegant dining is provided in King Stefan's Banquet Hall, within.
© Walt Disney Productions.

This is the part of Walt Disney World which is usually dismissed as a mere moneymaker. The serious visionary part is supposed to be EPCOT—a plan currently in the vague stage. The Magic Kingdom is not seriously considered as a possible model in its own right for city-planning of the future.

I think it is important, however. It suits the American mood. It has the smell and feel of an idea whose time has come.

135, 136. Two pneumatic structures by Frei Otto. An ellipsoid surrounded by a ring of domes, and two conical structures which would enliven the landscape no end!

In the Walt Disney World, The Magic Kingdom is a continual unfolding of artful stage-settings. In this way it resembles the dramatic cities of the past that we so admire, like Athens, Venice or Florence. For many centuries we have tried to copy those cities, piecemeal or entire, usually in vain. Their qualities don't seem to translate into a modern idiom. In spite of our best efforts modern cities are visually uninspired and uninspiring. The artistic schemes of our city-planners are unsatisfying on a man-in-the-street level. What is to be done?

The obvious is always difficult to see: architectural harmony and beauty must be based upon the popular forms of our times, just as Periclean Athens or Augustan Rome were based on the popular forms of their times. But these forms must be genuinely popular. They will probably not be the work of 'fine' artists of the day, since fine art is still an elitist interest. The popular (not Pop) art of our day has been made by men like Al Capp and Norman Rockwell, it is exhibited monthly in Heavy Metal Magazine, we see it in the myriad styles of advertising art, and most especially in the work of Walt Disney.

Popular taste is a liking for what is currently popular, whether it is Shakespeare, or Pericles, or Walt Disney. The popular is always considered vulgar; but today we are becoming less self-conscious about our taste. Every year, fewer and fewer people believe that they must prefer Rembrandt to Rockwell and Cézanne to Capp, or else be condemned as utter slobs. It is becoming possible nowadays to like the popular art of our own time simply and directly, without either apology or self-congratulation.

137. The exciting exterior of le Centre Pompidou in Paris, showing the external elevator. It is a building which has aroused much controversy, but no one can deny that it is fun.

138. A spacious open-plan version of the future from 1895, strictly for the genteel and elegant.

AVGVSTA:

A BIRD'S EYE

VIEW.

So why not consider Walt Disney World seriously? The architecture gives more pleasure to more people per year than Versailles. And the over-all plan is exceptionally promising, since it makes all of the areas of a city into prime and desirable locations.

Most cities have only one or two interesting 'regions', if that. These regions are their prime attractions: London's West End, New York's Greenwich Village, Paris's Left Bank, and so on. These desirable regions are always embedded in a vast expanse of dreary city-matter—blocks of uninteresting apartments and office buildings, visually dull, void of entertainment value, unpleasant to live in. These are the off-stage parts of cities, and they occupy the greatest area.

In Walt Disney World, as in Venice, there are no off-stage bits. Everything is on-stage, everything is worthy of visual consideration. Nor is there only a single interesting region In Walt Disney World, there are six centers within one small city. Following this principle, the multi-theme city of the future would be composed of many special quarters and districts and neighborhoods. What matter if they are artificial? Anything planned is artificial, until it is a few hundred or thousand years old, after which it somehow becomes natural, or even inevitable.

Walt Disney World is architecture for the people. The costumed actors, gotten up to look like Mickey Mouse or Donald Duck are vital. They reinforce the statement that each region makes, instill mood, embody a situation. They are the masked gods of the religion of fun, and they walk among the populace.

Having noted some of the welcome features of Walt Disney World, mention must also be made of its deficiencies. At present, Walt Disney World is designed for spectators only. To make a true city out of it, there must be participation. One way to achieve this: pass a law that would require all inhabitants of The Magic Kingdom to assume costumes in keeping with their region. There is ample historical precedent for this. Rather than wearing the chiton of Athens or the toga of Rome, Magic Kingdomers would dress up as one of the Seven Dwarfs, or some other mythological character within Disney's pantheon. This might not be absolutely necessary for everyday; but it would be useful for the modern fun equivalent of religious or regional festivals. It might feel a little strange at first; but after a few generations, Snow White and the Wizard of Oz would be recognized as important archetypal figures, of more relevance to us than Agamemnon or Clytemnestra.

Even if the problem of aesthetics could be solved, Walt Disney World is still a fragile place, dependent upon prosperity and favorable conditions for its continued success. Its growth must be slow and orderly, or the whole thing will go to pot. How would Walt Disney World handle the sort of demographic accident that all cities are subject to? As a regular American township rather than a private enterprise entertainment complex, the Magic Kingdom might have to face an unexpected influx of disadvantaged peoples. Suppose five or ten thousand exiled Guatemalans decided to settle here, with their own national dances, festivals, educational needs, and the like. Would Fairyland exist long in the face of real human necessity?

A more serious problem is: who will rule the Magic Fun Townships of the future? Democracy as we know it would be fatal to the concept. What if a determined minority wanted to raise an exhibit to Ming the Merciless, or Barbarella, or Felix the Cat? What if they wanted saloons and whorehouses on Main Street, pornographic movie houses on Liberty Square, and a Center for the Performing Arts in Frontiersville? Obviously it would never do. Walt Disney World is the work of a modern Lorenzo the Magnificent; an elected city manager could never be expected to keep it up.

139. Panorama for courting couples from two hundred floors up in Greater New York as imagined in the thirties.

Facing page
142.   A French desert city designed to look like a
barren outcrop of rock. The pilots are not de-
ceived, however. Mezières in Metal Hurlant.

140, 141.   Two architectural visions by the Italian
Futurist Sant'Elia, designed in the early part of
this century. Their proportions and elegance
strongly recall the Renaissance cities of Northern
Italy.

143. Robert Wolff brandishing the magic horn on the cover of the UK edition of the first volume in The World of the Tiers trilogy.

Disneyland has obvious limitations as a prototype fun city of the future. Is there any plan which will give us a truly different life? Can we conceive of a city, no matter how far-fetched, that will change our condition qualitatively?

I think the beginnings of such a vision are present in the four novels that make up Philip Jose Farmer's World of Tiers. In the first book, Maker of Universes, an Earthman named Robert Wolff gains possession of a magical horn. When blown with the right combination of notes, this horn enables Wolff to enter another world. It is a strange and beautiful place, populated by hybrid beasts, some of distant Earth ancestry, others completely alien. The people living in this world speak a pre-Homeric Greek which Wolff, luckily enough, is able to understand.

Wolff learns that this world was created by a being named Jadawin. Jadawin, and the 10,000 others of his race, lived in a universe parallel to Earth's. They were humanoids, but possessing great lifespan and incredible powers. Masters of science and technology, they were able to build complete planets and even universes to suit their desires. Despite millenia of warfare with an alien race, these Lords, as they are called, carry on an intense and murderous competition among themselves. The creator of this particular world is absent; a usurper Lord has managed to kill or put down all the competition and rule alone. To preserve his own life, Wolff will have to depose or kill this usurper.

Wolff finds himself in an artificially created world which is made up of tiers—continent-sized rectangular sections stacked one above another and imbedded into a gigantic monolith. The tiers are 30,000 feet apart and it is possible literally to fall off the edge of one of them. The various levels are connected by hidden 'gates', which can be opened with the magical horn. Each tier has its own characteristics and its own population. The tier Wolff enters is a reconstruction of pre-historic North America, and is populated by centaurs and American Indian tribes. Below this is the Atlantis level, and below that a Germanic world called Dracheland. At the topmost level dwells the Lord himself. Wolff goes through an amazing series of adventures and transformations. I will not reveal the conclusion.

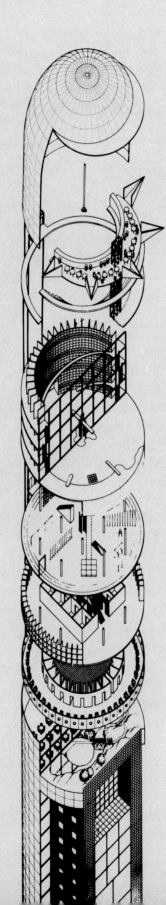

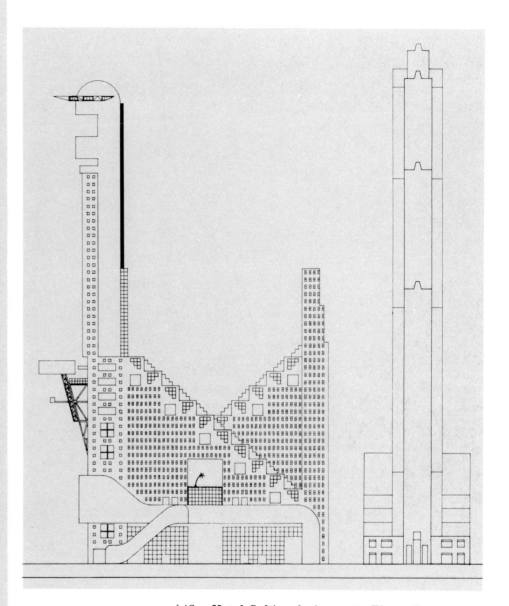

145.   Hotel Sphinx facing onto Times Square.

Left

144.   Hotel Sphinx, an idealised project by Elia Zenghelis: a luxury hotel that presents an ideal model for housing. The flanks of the structure are residential accommodation. The head of the Sphinx is dedicated to the sensual activities of physical culture and relaxation, with swimming pool, gymnasium, baths and beauty parlor, restaurant and English garden. The collective facilities are offered to the mixed population that occupies it, some of it transient, but mostly permanent. Once you've arrived, you need never leave.

SERENIS, WATER CITY OF CALLISTO

The people of Callisto love beauty, and their city is built on
a lake. It is the Venice of the outer worlds. See page 145.

Farmer's World of Tiers can be likened superficially to Disneyworld, and to its science-fictional equivalent, Futureworld, written by Mayo Simon and George Schenck and adapted by John Ryder Hall. Futureworld is about a Disney-style holiday resort called Delos, which is made up of Roman World, Medieval World, Spa World, and Futureworld. Costumed robots occupy each of these settings, and are available to the tourists for violence or sex.

These three worlds have a structural similarity. All three are arrays of interconnected regions, each logically consistent only to itself. Disneyworld and Futureworld differ from each other only in degree. In Disneyworld you walk among the actors, looking and listening, but you aren't allowed to touch. In Futureworld you are encouraged to 'participate'—to make love to the actors, or to kill them. But it still is only make-believe, for the actors are only machines.

Farmer's World of Tiers, the most fantastic of the three, is the only one to provide a framework for true participation. It conjures up a vision of mankind's future evolution, when we shall become as gods and live together in Ultimate City. Indeed, many legends claim that this was our state before we fell into 'single vision and Newton's sleep.'

Telepathy, clairvoyance, precognition, psychokinetics, teleportation, levitation, astral travel, all may be aspects and attributes of that state, momentary glimpses of the next step in our evolution. What will that next step be like? Among other things, it may involve our understanding of the simultaneity of all places and times, our perception of the instantaneous interconnectedness of all parts of the universe with each other and with ourselves. These may seem far-out considerations, but they are scientifically respectable. They are drawn from the writings of Einstein, Eddington, Heisenberg, Whitehead, and Shrodinger, among many others.

They give us a glimpse of the next level of our evolution, when we will be able directly to experience the universe as simultaneous n-dimensional space-time, with all places and times co-existent with ourselves. At this level, time, effort and distance will no longer exist, and Ultimate City will come spontaneously into being.

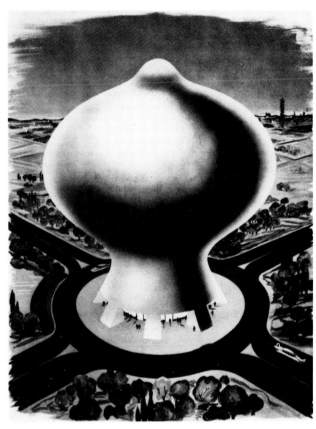

147. An extremely stately pleasure dome, designed by Nicolas Schöffer as a Centre for Sexual Pastimes, where a lot of fun could be yours for the asking.

Facing page
146. Serenis, the Venice of the Outer Worlds.

Galaxy

SCIENCE FICTION

APRIL 1951

25¢

ANC

INSIDE EARTH

By Poul Anderson

Above
149. City below the Moon's surface, by Robert McCall. Reduced gravity makes possible a dream-like movement through an idyllic environment. Columns provide elevator transport to the surface.

Facing page
148. An underground city illuminated by arc lights set into bedrock. Everybody travels on foot except for the people in the command module, who go up and down looking for irregularities.

Facing page
151. Mekonta, another Venice-inspired water world, this one on Venus. Note the humorless automatons trying to find their way to the repair shops.

What would life be like in Ultimate City? In some respects it would probably be much like human life anywhere at any time. You would most likely wake up in the morning, kiss the wife and kids goodbye, and go to your job. Even gods must want to settle down and get some work done. Despite your vast understanding and miraculous powers, or because of them, you doubtless would want regularity in your life, and the challenge of something useful to do. Your life would have restraints, but they would be self-chosen. And when you felt the need for new challenges, people, sights and sounds, you would move on, to a different part of town.

Ultimate City is the instantaneous interconnection within yourself of all points and times in the universe. Everything is equi-distant and equi-available, and it is all inside the city limits. You can step out of your door and into Ming China, or Hawaii in the last century, or Aldeberan yesterday, or Mars a thousand years ago. Wherever you go, you will see the familiar faces of the other inhabitants of the universe. Whatever you do will be useful work, since in Ultimate City everything has to be done.

150. Barnum Jnr's Magnificent and Fabulous City. Built on a scale five times smaller than reality, the city lies beneath a red and blue striped circus tent. It contains reproductions of all the major monuments in the world. When you arrive, you choose a character you'd like to be, and donning a special garment which transmits every movement of your body to the replica robot-doll you have chosen, you can enact any dreams or fantasies. You can do anything you want – nothing is forbidden.

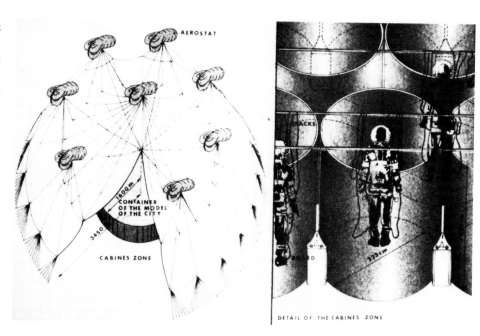

THREEPENCE

EVERY FRIDAY

EAGLE

21 JULY 1950 No 15

DAN DARE
PILOT OF THE FUTURE

HERE WE ARE, GENTLEMEN, THE FINEST CITY ON VENUS!

MEKONTA *Capital of the Northern Hemisphere of Venus*
A CITY BUILT ON FLOATING ISLANDS IN AN ARTIFICIALLY CALMED LAKE, AND CRISS-CROSSED BY CANALS FILLED WITH THE VARI-COLOURED WATER OF VENUS. THE HOME OF THE TREENS — HUMOURLESS SCIENTIFIC AUTOMATONS WHO RULE THE NORTHERN HALF OF THE MYSTERY PLANET.

FRANK HAMPSON

152. A sprightly and baroque conception of what we are coming to. The turrets provide welcome architectural contrast, and the long S-curve of the elevated railroad holds the masterpiece together.

153. Castles in the air, by Cruikshank. A fair and witty commentary on city speculations past and present.

ACKNOWLEDGMENTS
The publishers gratefully acknowledge the co-operation and
copyright permissions of the following in compiling the
material for this book (figures refer to illustrations):
Ace Books 46; Archigram 5, 102, 108, 109, 112, 125;
Architectural Review 96, 97; Arrow Books 88, 112;
Ballantine Books 23; The Bettmann Archive Inc 152;
Dargaud Editeur 48, 49, 71, 72, 93, 100; Mary Evans Picture
Library 3, 24, 66, 138, 153; Fratelli Fabbri 140, 141; Folio 53,
76, 130, 154; Hamlyn Books 1, 92; Alan Hutchings 33;
Institut fur leichte Flächentragwerke 7, 91; IPC 12, 17, 57,
151; Kunsthistorisches Museum Vienna 8; Robert McCall
64, 84, 94, 95, 106, 149; Cliff McReynolds 44; Metal Hurlant
2, 31, 60, 74, 142; MGM 34, 86, 133; F W Murnau-Stiftung
and Transit Film 112, 117; Novosti Press Agency 13, 20, 33,
43; Office of Metropolitan Architecture 144, 145; Frei Otto
85, 135, 136; Piano & Rodgers 137; Pilkington Brothers Ltd
55; Alex Raymond 122, 123; Scala 6, 25; Science Fiction
Foundation; Paolo Soleri 52, 61, 99; Space Frontiers Ltd 50,
51, 68, 69; Sphere Books 142; Superstudio 1971 4, 22, 59, 77,
76, 79, 80, 81, 82, 111, 120, 123, 150; Kenzo Tange 26, 27;
Trewin Copplestone Ltd 70; Walt Disney Productions 132,
133; Jerry Webb, Young Artists 10, 13, 15, 16, 41, 45, 63, 86,
97.

The publishers would like to thank Cassell & Co Ltd for
permission to quote from Archigram, Editor Peter Cook,
and Jonathan Cape and William Morrow Inc for permission
to quote from The High Frontier by Gerard K O'Neill.

For permission to reproduce material from Amazing and
Fantastic magazines we would like to thank Ultimate
Publishing Corporation (Amazing-Fantastic Publications), for
material from Astounding and Analog © 1937, 1950 by
Street and Smith Publications Inc renewed © 1962, 1965,
1978 by The Condé Nast Publications Inc we would like to
thank the Condé Nast Publications Inc.

The publishers would also like to thank all the other artists,
architects and companies who could not be traced in the
course of preparing this book for publication.

Cover design by Alan Daniels

Overleaf
154. What Lies Ahead by George Underwood.